W9-CID-679

THE GREEKS IN AMERICA

THE GREEKS

IN AMERICA

Jayne Clark Jones

 Lerner Publications Company · Minneapolis

Front cover: The Chris Kalogerson Greek-American dance band, based in Minneapolis, uses the bouzouki (a stringed instrument) and the folk clarinet to produce an authentic Greek sound. From left to right are Andros Antoniades (from Cyprus), Jim Roth, Callie Kalogerson, Chris Kalogerson, and Christos Christodoulou (also from Cyprus).

Page 2: Representative Nicholas Mavroules of Massachusetts is one of many Greek-Americans in the U.S. House of Representatives.

1990 REVISED EDITION

The Library of Congress cataloged the original printing of this title as follows:

Jones, Jayne Clark.
  The Greeks in America. Minneapolis, Lerner Publications Co. [1969]

  78 p. illus., facsim., maps, ports. 24cm. (The In America Series)

  Traces the history of Greek emigration from classical times to the present day with emphasis on the problems of Greek immigrants in the United States and their contributions to America's history and culture.

  1. Greeks in the United States—Juvenile literature. [1. Greeks in the United States] I. Title.

E184.G7J6   301.453′495′073   68-31504
ISBN 0-8225-0215-1 [Library Edition]   MARC
ISBN 0-8225-1010-3 [Paper Edition]   AC

Manufactured in the United States of America

6 7 8 9 10 11 12 13 14 15 99 98 97 96 95 94 93 92 91 90

CONTENTS

1 ANCIENT WAYFARERS 6
The Hellenic Heritage   6
The First Greek Emigrants   9
Alexander and a New Era of Greek Emigration   11
The Eastern Roman Empire (Byzantium)   12
Greeks under the Ottomans   15

2 WEST OF ATLANTIS 16
The Earliest Greeks in America   16
The Century of Revolt   20
Greek Refugees in America   23
Problems after Independence   26

3 THE IMMIGRANTS 30
Motives and Expectations   30
Obstacles in America   31
The Padrones   35
A Variety of Solutions   36
Repatriation   42
Turmoil in the Homeland   42
Survival of Hellenic Culture   51

4 CONTRIBUTIONS TO AMERICAN LIFE 52
Government   52
Business   54
Science and Education   58
Literature, Music, and Art   60
Entertainment and Sports   65

INDEX 69
ACKNOWLEDGMENTS 71

1
ANCIENT WAYFARERS

The columns of the Temple of Hephaestus in Athens show the simple, clean lines of the Doric style of architecture–one of many Greek styles that have influenced American architects.

The Hellenic Heritage

For the United States, Greece can never be just another faraway country. Many public buildings and great structures in the United States have been built to resemble ancient Greek temples. Our dictionaries are full of Greek words. Our museums contain Greek pottery and sculpture. Even beginning students of philosophy know something about Plato and Aristotle, and students of poetry learn about Homer, Pindar, and Sappho. Plays by Aeschylus, Sophocles, or Euripides are still staged. College fraternities and sororities have Greek names.

Of all the things we have borrowed from ancient Greek civilization, one of the most highly valued is the form of government chosen by Thomas Jefferson and the founders of our country. We still call it by its Greek name: democracy. For these reasons the United States has always been especially interested in the affairs of Greece.

The Greeks call themselves Hellenes and call their country Hellas. Many words related to Greece and Greeks are built from this root word. *Panhellenic* means "related to all the Greeks." A *philhellene* is someone who

This Minnesota family is descended from Greeks who came to the United States in the early 20th century.

loves Greece and Greek culture. To *hellenize* something means to make it more Greek.

The United States has been hellenized to some extent—not only by the influence of ancient writers and thinkers but also by many modern Greeks who have become Americans. Just under 700,000 Greeks immigrated to the United States from 1820 (the first year in which immigrants' nationalities were recorded) through 1989, according to the U.S. Immigration and Naturalization Service. In the 1980 U.S. census, 959,856 persons reported having at least partial Greek ancestry.

These numbers are relatively small, especially in comparison to the numbers of immigrants from other parts of Europe. For example, German immigrants to the United States have outnumbered Greek immigrants by about 10 to 1. Even though the United States has been a favorite destination of emigrating Greeks, the number of Greeks who could move to America has been limited by several things.

Some of these limitations have been imposed by Greek governments. During the Balkan Wars (1912-1913), for example, the Greek government would not allow the emigration of men who could serve in the army. Through most of history, however, the Greek authorities have been happy to let people of working age emigrate to America and send part of their wages back to their families in Greece.

Distribution of Greek-Americans in the U.S., 1980

New York	160,569	Texas	24,320
California	107,074	Connecticut	23,907
Illinois	88,324	Virginia	17,959
Massachusetts	76,170	Indiana	15,637
New Jersey	53,831	Wisconsin	12,615
Pennsylvania	51,888	Washington	12,261
Ohio	46,655	New Hampshire	11,381
Florida	41,022	Missouri	10,363
Michigan	39,386	North Carolina	10,223
Maryland	26,204	Colorado	9,881

Source: U.S. Dept. of Commerce, Bureau of the Census (1980), from an overall U.S. total of 959,856 persons reporting Greek ancestry

Other limitations have been imposed by the United States. For about 40 years, from the mid-1920s to the mid-1960s, Greek immigration was limited to a quota of 308 persons a year. The Greek quota was part of a strict immigration system resulting from prejudice, especially against Mediterranean and Oriental peoples, in America during the 1920s. Despite the restrictions, however, about 56,000 Greeks entered the country outside the quota—some as refugees after World War II, some as returnees who had been trapped by World War II while visiting relatives in Greece, and some as students during the 1950s.

In 1965 a new immigration system that did away with the old quotas went into effect. The law limited immigration from Eastern Hemisphere nations to 170,000 persons a year—regardless of their homeland—with a maximum of 20,000 from any one nation. During the 1980s, an average of about 3,600 Greeks immigrated to the United States each year.

The modern Greek influence in the United States is prominent despite the modest numbers of immigrants. Greek-Americans generally maintain a strong sense of their ancestral culture. Family, religion, and the Greek language have been focal points for Greek-Americans. A sense of community strengthened the Greeks when, like many other immigrant groups, they faced hardship and prejudice. This cultural identity survived even after the Greeks established themselves as leading citizens throughout the United States.

Greek-Americans have distinguished themselves in literature, films, medicine, science, politics, sports, and nearly every other field of endeavor. This modern form of hellenization has benefited the United States in countless ways—a testimony to the talents of the Greeks in America.

The First Greek Emigrants

The reason for Greek emigration is to be found in the geography of Greece itself. Mainland Greece is a small peninsular country with an enormously long, irregular coastline. The land that can be cultivated is divided into fairly small parcels by very high, rugged mountains. The mountains and the sea give Greece its special beauty and determine its way of life. Roads through the mountains have always been few and dangerous, so people have traveled over them as little as possible. For this reason, the inland areas of Greece have always been isolated from each other.

But no one is very far from the main highway of Greece, the sea. With agricultural land scarce and poor, Greece has faced the same problem again and again: too many people for the resources of the land. The sea provided a way out for the Greeks. Those with too little could sail away. Others could bring back food and goods for those who remained.

Long before classical times (500-400 B.C.) the people of Greece had organized their society around what we now call city-states. The largest town or city of a region was the center of government, politics, and culture in the area. But the populations of these little states soon outgrew the ability of the land to support them. Too many people with too little to eat will, sooner or later, disrupt the order of any society.

As early as the eighth century B.C., the city-states of ancient Greece had begun to solve their problems of political discontent and overpopulation by sending out their citizens as colonists. The emigrants were bound to the home city by ties of loyalty and affection—they traditionally started a new hearth in each colony with sacred fire carried from a hearth in their home city—but they were completely free to seek their fortunes and govern themselves in a new land.

The Parthenon, a temple to the goddess Athena, was built during the Golden Age of Athens in the fifth century B.C.

Alexander the Great conducted an amazingly successful campaign of conquest, spreading Greek culture through much of northeast Africa and southwest Asia.

The colonists went everywhere the sea would take them. They settled and traded in Sicily, in southern Italy, and in France, along the fringes of Asia Minor, the Black Sea, and Africa, and among all the islands in between. They carried their language and culture with them, sometimes hellenizing their neighbors.

By 450 B.C., because of their colonies and trade, the Greek city-states dominated the Mediterranean world. The greatest city-state of them all was Athens. Here, for the first time in history, a great state was governed by somewhat democratic means. The mighty Athenian navy regulated trade on the Mediterranean and demanded tribute, or payment, from the states that it controlled. As a cultural center, Athens attracted artists, philosophers, scientists, and writers, as well as their students. During the fifth century B.C., the Parthenon was built on the Athenian acropolis. Athens set the standards of style and beauty for the entire Greek-influenced Mediterranean.

It was not easy, however, to be a world power. Old rivals led by the city-state of Sparta began a war against Athens that lasted for nearly 30 years. A firm and united government might have saved Athens, but its leaders quarreled among themselves and disagreed about what action to take. Their uncertain policy was fatal. When Athens finally surrendered in 404 B.C., its navy had been destroyed and its empire broken up. Without sea power, Athens could no longer remain dominant in the area.

But the long ruinous war had also weakened the other great city-states. Although groups of city-states had once united in leagues for protection and trade—and had managed to keep peace for religious festivals and for such athletic contests as the original Olympics—they were never able to achieve the panhellenic union that might have saved them. Eventually a new power came to rule over the Greek-speaking people.

Alexander and a New Era of Greek Emigration

To the north of Greece lay the independent kingdom of Macedonia. Under its powerful and clever king, Philip II (382-336 B.C.), Macedonia was able to gain control of the city-states of Greece. Philip spoke Greek, had a Greek education, and knew how to take advantage of the quarrels among the Greeks. He kept them weak by encouraging and even provoking disputes among them.

After Philip was assassinated at an early age, his young son Alexander inherited control of the army. The army was a very good one composed of Macedonians and mercenary Greek soldiers. Instead of trying to subdue all the Greeks who continued to scheme and plot against him, Alexander set out for the coast of Asia Minor to free Greek lands and people from Persian rule. Many of the Greeks there responded by halting their disputes and following Alexander in his campaign against the Persians.

Phenomenally successful, he became known as Alexander the Great. He marched through country after country in Africa and Asia: Egypt, Syria, Palestine, Babylon, Persia, all the way to

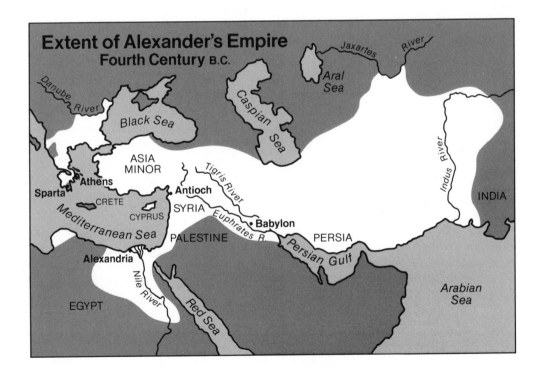

Extent of Alexander's Empire
Fourth Century B.C.

India. Finally his army, tired of years of campaigning, threatened mutiny. Alexander turned back, but he only got as far as Babylon, where in 323 B.C. he died of a fever at the age of 33. He had not lived long enough to organize his vast empire, but his armies left the mark of Greece throughout the East. Alexander had rewarded his soldiers with gifts of land in the conquered territory if they would make their homes there and guard the new lands. Many veterans took advantage of this.

After Alexander died, his lands were divided among several of his generals. They encouraged colonists to come and strengthen the new Greek cities in the East. The city-states of Greece were again overpopulated. So were many Greek cities in Asia Minor, some of which had themselves begun as colonies from the mainland. So, Greek settlers left them to go farther east to the new frontiers or to settle in Egypt. They spread their language and culture as they went.

Alexander's successors and the dynasties (ruling families) they founded reigned for nearly 200 years. In many of the more remote parts of Asia conquered by Alexander's forces, Greek influence eventually waned. But in other lands near the sea or on trade routes, in the newer cities (such as Alexandria and Antioch) established by Alexander's followers, and even in many older cities in Egypt and Syria, society had become truly Greek.

This hellenistic influence remained even after the dynasties founded by Alexander's generals had lost power. The rulers, merchants, artists, craftspersons, and professionals were all Greek. The non-Greek native people remained only as peasants or shepherds in the lowest classes of society. Common Greek (or *koine*) was the language of commerce. In art, science, philosophy, and literature the Greeks of the East made great contributions to Greek culture. This Greek world was the one into which the new power of Rome began to expand in the second century B.C.

The Eastern Roman Empire (Byzantium)

Through 200 B.C., the Macedonians continued to manipulate the city-states of mainland Greece, and the Greeks resented it. When the Greeks invited the Romans to be their allies against Philip V, they were thinking only of being free of Macedonian meddling. The Romans promised to protect Greek freedom and independence, but they soon began their own rigid rule in Greece.

Then the Romans invaded the East, swallowing one country after another. After each conquest, the vanquished region became part of the Roman imperial system. When the tribal people of the French and German forests had been conquered, the Roman concepts of city life, political bureaucracy, and

The Byzantine church of Hagia Sophia (Divine Wisdom) in Istanbul, Turkey, was built in the sixth century, when the Byzantine Empire was at its peak.

centralized power came as something entirely new. In the hellenized East, Roman ways were far less novel.

The Romans had long been in awe of Greek culture. Greek traders had been selling beautiful artifacts to the tribes of Italy when Rome was just a country town. Well-educated Romans knew both Latin and Greek and were well acquainted with Greek literature. They often chose Greek slaves to tutor their children. They sent their older sons to Athens, Rhodes, Pergamum, and Alexandria for their "university" education in oratory, philosophy, medicine, and science. Roman rule had very little effect on the complex, sophisticated city life of the East.

But the empire was too big to handle. Enemies within and enemies without kept Rome at war year after year. When Roman power began to give way to repeated barbarian attacks from all sides, the hellenized eastern part of the Roman Empire proved to be the most stable.

In A.D. 395, the Roman Empire was divided into two parts. Rome was the capital of the western half and Constantinople, which the Roman Emperor Constantine had been using as his capital for a number of years, was the eastern capital. The eastern part of the empire was called the Byzantine Empire because the Greek name of the capital city had been Byzantium before Constantine changed it. The Byzantine emperors considered themselves Roman, but their language, culture, officials, and citizens were Greek.

An Ottoman sultan holds court in Istanbul. Even though the sultan had ultimate authority in the empire, he needed a huge organization of advisers and civil servants to assist him. Many of these officials were Greeks who had helped govern the Byzantine Empire.

The Byzantine Empire marks the greatest extent of Greek power in history. The Byzantine Greeks became the traders of the Mediterranean world. The Byzantine navy protected commerce on the high seas. Constantinople itself formed the hub of trade routes that linked the Far East and the West. Because of their wealth, powerful cities, and secure government, the Byzantines were able to survive many of the pressures that forced the collapse of the Roman Empire in the West.

Increasingly, even before the western part of the empire succumbed to invasions by tribes from the north, the two parts of the empire drifted apart. Byzantium and Rome quarreled and fought over territorial and religious matters. Disputes about the authority structure within Christianity led to a split between the Eastern Christians and the church of Rome—and to the formation of the Eastern Orthodox Church.

But the Byzantine Empire did not survive as a strong, unified whole throughout its existence. It suffered invasions by Slavs and Avars from the north and by Persians from the east. Finally, after the death of the prophet Mohammed in A.D. 632, the Islamic peoples began a prolonged assault that eventually ended in the complete destruction of the Byzantine Empire. The Arabs began whittling away the provinces of Syria, Palestine, Egypt, and North Africa. The Ottoman Turks ended it all in 1453 by capturing Constantinople.

By the time they finally conquered Constantinople in 1453, the well-trained troops of the Ottoman Empire had already occupied much of Greece.

Greeks under the Ottomans

The early Turkish sultans were capable rulers. They recognized that the Ottoman Turks, a small minority in their conquered territory, did not have the power or experience to govern their unwieldy empire. Needing the talents and skills of the people they had conquered, the sultans turned to the Greeks, who had considerable administrative talent. Greeks in other walks of life—farmers, fishermen, sailors, and merchants—went on very much as they had under Byzantine rule. Some Jews and members of other religions were even relieved by the Turkish policy of religious tolerance.

In 1453, when Constantinople fell to the Turks, the nations of western Europe were on the verge of a great age of discovery, exploration, and colonization. But the Turks were less motivated than the French or Portuguese or English to venture out upon the seas. The Ottoman Empire controlled the trade routes from the East, so they needed no elaborate trans-Atlantic passage to the Orient. Their ambition was to expand into Europe, and they were not interested in claiming new lands across the seas.

Their Turkish overlords might have lacked interest in exploratory seafaring, but Greek-speaking people were still a part of the maritime world. Very early in the records of the Spanish expeditions to the New World the names of Greek sailors, pilots, captains, and merchants can be found.

2
WEST OF ATLANTIS

Greeks were early participants in the European exploration of the New World. One Greek sailor, listed simply as "John," accompanied Christopher Columbus.

The Earliest Greeks in America

In classical times, Greek stories (borrowed from the Egyptians) told of an advanced and prosperous island kingdom that suddenly sank into the sea and was completely destroyed. When Plato wrote about this kingdom, called Atlantis, he placed it far to the west, in the Atlantic Ocean. If such a kingdom ever existed, it was probably not where Plato said it was, but Greeks of a more modern seafaring era were poised to cross the waters that had seemed so unimaginably distant in Plato's time.

In 1527, the king of Spain gave to a Spanish nobleman, Narváez, a grant to all the Florida lands previously discovered by Ponce de Leon and Juan de Garay. The story of Narváez's travels during the 1530s tells of a Greek sailor named Theodore who was with him. When the expedition was near present-day Pensacola and in desperate need of fresh water, Native Americans ferried it out on rafts to the ship. Theodore insisted on helping during one trip to shore to get more water; though the Native Americans returned to the ship, Theodore didn't. In 1540, when DeSoto's expedition was passing through Alabama, the native peoples of the area told him about a Christian who had been there from the time of Narváez. Although this Christian was reportedly no longer alive, DeSoto was shown a dagger that supposedly had belonged to this man. The adventurous Theodore may have been the first Greek to set foot on American soil.

A number of Greeks are listed in the chronicles of various Spanish explorers in the New World. A Greek sailor named John sailed with Columbus. Magellan had three Greeks with him when he went through what were later named the Straits of Magellan, at the tip of South America. When Sir Francis Drake, in 1578, and Thomas Cavendish, in 1588, first arrived on the west coast of South America, they were able to hire Greek pilots who were thoroughly familiar with the waters off Chile and Peru.

During these years, the sea rivalry between the Spanish and the English was very fierce. When Drake and Cavendish appeared on the west coast of New Spain, the Spanish believed that these Englishmen had somehow found the Northwest Passage. The English had actually sailed around South America just as the Spanish had. Still, their presence in the Pacific unnerved the Spaniards, who were determined to find and blockade the western outlet of the supposed Northwest Passage, which they called the Straits of Anian.

Dr. Andrew Turnbull founded the colony of New Smyrna in Florida. Many of the colonists he recruited were Greeks.

The Straits of Juan de Fuca, between Vancouver Island and the state of Washington, were named after a Greek explorer.

The viceroy of Mexico organized an expedition of three ships and 100 troops and entrusted them to a Greek sailor whom they called Juan de Fuca. De Fuca had been employed by the Spanish for 40 years and had been in the West Indies, California, and the Philippines. He had even been robbed of his personal fortune when Cavendish stopped and plundered his ship off the coast of California. De Fuca's first attempt to find the straits failed when his soldiers mutinied, but in 1592 he was asked to try again with only one ship. He sailed north along the coast of California and beyond until he entered a broad channel, which he followed as far as the 47th or 48th degree of north latitude. He was convinced that he had found his goal, but because he

was worried about the fur-clad people whom he had seen on the shores, he went no farther. He expected a great reward for his accomplishment, but the viceroy had only praise, not gold, for him. De Fuca then went to Spain where, again, he hoped to be rewarded, but his only reward was a little public recognition and a reception by the king. Disillusioned and broke, he headed for home, the island of Cephalonia off the western coast of Greece.

In Venice, on his way to Greece, de Fuca met the English diplomat Michael Lok and described his voyages. He convinced Lok that England could use someone like him in the English quest for the Northwest Passage. But, while Lok was trying to make arrangements with English officials for money and ships, de Fuca died. The descriptions that de Fuca gave Lok indicate that he had sailed into the straits that separate Vancouver Island from the state of Washington. In 1725, the Russian Imperial Academy of Science named these straits for him—the Straits of Juan de Fuca.

Greek names, or names with "greco" or "griego" attached to them, appear in numerous records of colonial America. Most people with such names were merchants or seafarers, such as the Captain Thomas Grecian who came to Boston from Ireland in 1660. His children had Greek names and he was probably a Greek. Unfortunately, since nothing is known of these people except their names in some public record, such clues are hard to follow further.

The first sizable settlement of Greeks in America took place in 1767 under rather unusual circumstances. Florida had become a British colony in 1763. An enterprising Scottish doctor named Andrew Turnbull obtained permission from the governor of Florida to work 20,000 acres of uncultivated land near St. Augustine. Under the terms of his contract with the government, Turnbull was to bring only Protestants to Florida. (The Orthodox Greek Christians qualified.)

Turnbull's wife was the daughter of a Greek general from Smyrna, and Turnbull himself was familiar with the Mediterranean area. He collected, as settlers to work his land, destitute and desperate people from Greece, Italy, Corsica, and Majorca. To induce them

Nineteenth-century visitors to the site of New Smyrna survey the ruins of the colony.

to come with him, he described Florida as a paradise and promised to make them landowners. He agreed to supply them with passage, food, and clothing for three years—and return passage if they wanted to leave after six months' trial. In addition, he agreed to give each family 50 acres of land and an additional 25 acres for each child in the family. He brought about 1,400 men, women, and children to the settlement, which he named New Smyrna in honor of his wife's home.

The voyage was terribly hard and many of the colonists died at sea, but even worse conditions awaited them in Florida. Instead of working vineyards and olive groves as they had been led to expect, they found themselves cultivating cotton in swampy, malaria-infested bottomlands and being harassed by hostile Native Americans. Furthermore, their work was directed by English overseers who knew none of the languages spoken by the colonists and who treated them cruelly.

When Turnbull's promises were not kept, the settlers finally realized that they were no better off than slaves. The leaders of one group who tried to escape to Cuba were executed. In the meantime, the governor who had granted Turnbull his charter had been replaced by another who was not on good terms with the doctor. The first colonists who left New Smyrna stole away secretly, but news of a sympathetic government and legal help in St. Augustine led to a mass exodus.

By 1777 the New Smyrna colony was completely deserted and the Turnbulls had gone to South Carolina. Of a total of 1,400 immigrants who were brought by Turnbull to Florida, only 600 survived the hardships to find freedom.

The Century of Revolt

The successful American and French revolutions of the late 1700s inspired the Spaniards, the Poles, Serbs, Greeks, and Latin Americans to seek national independence in the 19th century. The idea of national autonomy was putting an end to empires.

The Turks had never been able (nor had they ever tried) to weld the diverse peoples of their empire into a nation. Each ethnic group remained distinct. As the empire aged, the vigor of the Turks declined. The later empire, after 1699, suffered from a long succession of incompetent sultans. With enemies pressing on all sides and an inadequate government, the Turks resorted to harsh, despotic methods to keep the empire functioning. Taxes became ruinous in many places. Citizens had no way to redress grievances against local Turkish authorities.

As their misery increased, the peoples of the Turkish empire rose in revolt in scattered areas. Whenever they did, they were put down with such violence that their resistance was intensified. Many Greeks escaped or were driven into the mountains, where they lived

The site of New Smyrna now looks pleasant and peaceful—in contrast to the conditions faced by the early Greek settlers. Disease and oppressive labor under Turnbull's overseers led many to flee the colony.

as bandits waging intermittent guerilla warfare on the Turkish authorities. Among the upper classes, secret revolutionary groups were formed, sometimes with the knowledge of the church. They sought the help of other nations and of important persons for the cause of Greek freedom. This was roughly the situation in 1821 at the beginning of the Greek War for Independence.

The United States had only recently finished its own revolution. The young American government was carefully feeling its way in the world, observing strict neutrality, trying to establish commercial relations with and recognition by other countries. Many of the leaders of the American Revolution,

however, regarded Greece as the cradle of democracy and republicanism and felt a deep debt to the Greeks of classical times. In addition, they were almost automatically in sympathy with the efforts of any nation to be free of the old imperial powers.

Because of exciting new archaeological excavations in Italy, a new interest in classical culture, both Greek and Roman, had arisen in western Europe and America. Classical style in art, architecture, and domestic design also enjoyed a revival. Many educated Americans were unusually interested in Greece at this time and were aware of the desperate condition of the modern Greeks and their desire for freedom.

The Greek War for Independence was a ferocious struggle between a small guerilla-style army and a larger, more conventional Turkish force. For Greece to be subdued, the Turks had to occupy the Peloponnesus, the southernmost region of the Greek mainland. Each time the Turkish army tried to march south along either coastline of this peninsula, they were hampered and harried over the rugged trails by the

21

Dr. Samuel Gridley Howe, an American philhellene, assisted the Greeks in their fight for independence from the Ottoman Empire. He also founded the Perkins Institute in Boston, a school for the blind.

Greeks. Although they had more success in some years than in others, the Turkish army never finished the job before the approach of winter forced them to withdraw again to their bases in the north.

The Greeks established a revolutionary government early in the war so that they would be prepared to assume power if they were successful in driving out the Turks. But once the government was established, political discord arose. The Greek military leaders fought each other over the location of the government (it moved often during these years), who should head it, who should be represented in it, and how it should be organized.

The Triple Alliance—Britain, France, and Russia—gave the Greeks some assistance and lots of sympathy, but these countries wanted no war with Turkey themselves, so they avoided an open alliance. Individual Americans came to Greece to help out as private citizens, but the Greeks needed and expected official aid from the United States government. None ever came. The U.S. Navy stationed ships in the Mediterranean throughout the war, but naval personnel never officially went into action on behalf of the Greeks. In fact, their secret mission was to try to establish trade with Turkey.

The U.S. government never changed its official position, but the American public collected a total of eight shiploads of food and supplies for the civilian refugees of the war. Other American individuals served with the Greek forces or contributed other services on a private basis. The Americans and other foreigners who devoted themselves to the cause of Greek liberty during the War for Independence were known as philhellenes. They included such prominent figures as the British poet Lord Byron (who died of an illness contracted while he was helping the Greeks).

Greek Refugees in America

The Greeks who came to the United States at this time were mainly children or young men of wealthy families whose relatives could afford to arrange their evacuation. Many orphans or refugees of the war were also sent to America by American philhellenes who found them in Greece. Most became successful in their chosen work and helped the cause of Greek-American friendship both here and abroad.

One of the most savage episodes of the War for Independence took place in 1822. Of the 100,000 Greek inhabitants of the island of Chios, all but 5,000 were either massacred or sold into slavery by the Turks. A number of children who survived the massacre were later sent to America. One of these, George M. Colvocoresses (1816-1872), later had a distinguished naval career in the United States as commander of the *USS Supply* and the *Saratoga* during the Civil War. He retired with the rank of captain. His son, George Partridge Colvocoresses, followed in his father's footsteps as a naval officer (in the Spanish-American War) and eventually attained the rank of rear admiral. Several other Greek-Americans of this period also served in the U.S. Navy.

Professor Evangelinos Apostolides Sophocles was born in Thessaly in eastern Greece. The Greek War of Independence interrupted his studies of the Greek classical period, but he continued them in Cairo and later on Syros (an island off the southern tip of Greece). His teacher on Syros teased him for being such a gifted student and gave him the nickname Sophocles. An American missionary invited him

Rear Admiral
George Partridge Colvocoresses

23

to go to the United States, where Sophocles arrived in 1828. In 1842, he joined Harvard College as a tutor in Greek and remained a member of the Harvard faculty until his death in 1883. He wrote several Greek grammars, but his great work was a Greek lexicon of over 1,000 pages. He was renowned as a brilliant eccentric who tended a flock of pet chickens that he named for friends and colleagues.

John Zachos (1820-1898) was the child of a Greek family that had been prominent in the Turkish government. His father, a member of a secret society that plotted revolution, escaped after having been betrayed to the Turks but was later killed while fighting in northern Greece. After the war, Zachos's mother was persuaded to send her son to America to be educated. He was trained as a physician but he never practiced medicine. He was co-principal of a girl's academy in Ohio for a while. After the Civil War, he supervised the welfare and education of some 600 former slaves who had been left destitute by their former masters. Later Zachos served as a minister and then as a professor of rhetoric. In 1871 he became curator of the Cooper Union, an institute for the advancement of arts and sciences, in New York City.

Colonel Lucas Miltiades Miller (1824-1902) was a war orphan who was adopted by Colonel J. P. Miller, an American who had fought with the Greek forces. Lucas M. Miller was educated in the law, and shortly after

Michael Anagnos, a Greek journalist who came to the United States to work with Dr. Samuel Gridley Howe, eventually married Howe's daughter and succeeded him as director of the Perkins Institute.

he was admitted to the bar he moved to Oshkosh, Wisconsin. He became a farmer there and took an active part in public affairs. He was a colonel during the Mexican War and was elected to Congress in 1891.

One of the greatest American philhellenes was Dr. Samuel Gridley Howe (1801-1876). He served as surgeon to the Greek rebel army, helped distribute the relief cargo sent to aid the Greek civilian refugees, and established hospitals in the new nation. Besides working in Greece between 1825 and 1831, he wrote and traveled in the United States to encourage Americans to aid the Greek cause.

After the war, he established the Perkins Institute, a school for the blind, in Boston. In 1861, Howe returned to Greece during the Cretan Revolution to direct the relief assistance for the Cretans. He hired as his secretary Michael Anagnos (1837-1906), a young Greek journalist, who eventually returned to the United States with him. Later, Anagnos worked as a teacher in the Perkins Institute, married Howe's only daughter, and, when Howe retired, became director of the institute. Under his direction, the institute took increased interest in the deaf blind. Ann Sullivan, the tutor who first helped Helen Keller, was sent to her from the Perkins Institute. Anagnos established a kindergarten for the blind, founded a press to print books for the blind, and developed programs to train the blind for jobs. Anagnos was also well known for the help he gave to Greek immigrants, his participation in the Greek community in Boston, and the efforts he made to help improve education in Greece.

Colonel Lucas Miltiades Miller lived in this large home on Lake Winnebago in Oshkosh, Wisconsin.

Problems after Independence

The task of restoring peace and order to Greece looked insurmountable. The leaders of the revolutionary forces had no experience in organizing a government, and they mistrusted the only Greeks with administrative experience—those who had been part of the Turkish government. The new government was paralyzed by disagreements among its leaders, and the country was devastated by the war and deeply in debt to the countries of the Triple Alliance.

After a while, the Greeks agreed to accept a foreign king to be chosen by the European powers. A Bavarian prince, Otho, was selected. Young, inexperienced, and ignorant of Greece and its problems, Otho not only did nothing to solve the country's postwar problems but actually made things worse. In 1844 Otho was forced to accept a constitution that allowed a representative government and curbed some of the worst abuses of royal power, but that was not enough.

In 1862 Otho was deposed. George I of Denmark took his place the following year. George allowed his Greek ministers to govern the country, and at last the real work of reconstruction began. Still, it went slowly.

After 400 years of stagnation under the Turks, Greece resembled a 15th-century nation when it began to rebuild in the last decades of the 19th century.

The government's attempts to modernize the country began to bring some prosperity, but mostly to the urban middle class. New railroads, a new navy, and new industry all meant progress and growth for the cities.

Greece, however, was mainly an agricultural country, and the depressed rural majority suffered on without even any way to make the government listen to their complaints. The old unjust land laws were never reformed. The rural population still carried an unfair share of the tax burden. While cities and railroads were being built, vital country roads were not even being repaired. Most of the country's money was being invested in high-profile modernization projects, and very little remained for rural areas.

Money for loans was available only at such high interest rates that no farmer could afford to borrow to make improvements. Once someone got into debt there was little chance of getting out. Caught in this financial squeeze, farmers could not educate their children or provide dowries for their daughters. Without education or advantageous marriages, the farmer's family was unlikely to improve its financial position. In addition, any natural disaster (such as an earthquake, drought, or flood) or any change in the usual markets for their produce could ruin many farmers.

When the Triple Alliance was drafting the treaty to end the War for Independence, Greece was given control over

Greece

The modern nation of Greece is much larger than Greece was at the time of independence from the Turks in 1832. At that time, only the mainland regions south of Thessaly and Epirus, as well as a group of islands just southeast of Athens, were under Greek rule. The Ionian Islands became part of Greece about 30 years later and Thessaly joined in the 1880s. The rest of Greece, however, remained under Turkish or Italian control. In 1913, with victory in the Balkan Wars, Greece greatly expanded to include Crete, Epirus, Macedonia, and some of the islands near Turkey (including Samos and Chios). Thrace became part of Greece after World War I. It was not until 1947, however, that modern Greece expanded to its present borders. In that year, the Italians ceded Rhodes and nearby islands to Greece.

Rural homes in Greece often housed a dozen people in one or two rooms. The hardships of life in Greece's countryside led many Greek farmers to seek prosperity in America.

only a small part of the Greek peninsula. This left more Greeks outside of Greece than inside. The Ionian Islands (off the west coast of Greece) were under British administration; the Aegean Islands were under Italian control. Almost everything else—northern Greece (Thessaly, Epirus, Macedonia), Crete, Cyprus, and the coastal area of Anatolia (including Smyrna and Constantinople)—was still in Turkish territory.

These lands, predominantly Greek but outside Greek sovereignty, were known as *unredeemed lands*. The Greek government was eager to recover this territory, but factions within the leadership could not agree on how to do so. Some leaders optimistically hoped that the unredeemed lands could be restored to Greece in time, by diplomatic means. Others dreamed of restoring the old Byzantine Empire and returning Greece to its ancient glory—by military means if necessary. The continual threat from Turkey forced Greece to maintain a state of military readiness, and occasional wars, such as the Greco-Turkish War of 1897, broke out. Many families suffered additional hardship when their men were drafted into military service.

Heavy taxation, scarce money, natural disasters, market failures, and threat of military service weighed most heavily on the rural poor. All of these things combined in various ways, year after year, to leave many Greek farmers without any opportunity to improve their lot or any hope for the future. So, in 1875, when Christos Tsankonas came back to Sparta from his first trip to the United States, his fellow Greeks were ready to listen to what he had to say. When he returned to the United States, five other Greeks went with him. In the decade between 1871 and 1880, 210 Greeks left for the United States. In the next 10 years, 2,308 followed them. The great flight from Greece had begun.

Greeks prepare to sail for America from the Greek port of Patras, on the northern Peloponnesus.

3
THE IMMIGRANTS

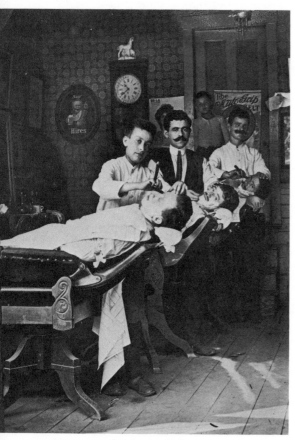

A rare photograph from 1910 shows a busy Greek-owned barbershop in the United States.

Motives and Expectations

Who were these Greeks who chose to gamble everything on a chance in the United States? As we have seen, the economic and political problems of Greece had their severest effects on the rural citizens. The emigrants were usually farmers in the productive years of their lives. Between 1880 and 1902, more than 90 percent were males. Most had family responsibilities and some land, livestock, or modest savings. They usually had only a little education. Their intentions were clear and simple: They wanted to earn enough money to solve their financial problems at home and were willing to exile themselves temporarily to do it. They left behind spouses, parents, and children. Most intended, once their debts were paid and they had saved a little to make life more comfortable, to go home again.

Most of the Greek immigrants tried to send money home as soon as they could, even if it meant borrowing some to enclose in their first letters. Plenty of letters from the United States told of hardship and unhappiness in

America, but these were more than offset by encouraging, positive, and hopeful letters—often containing cash. The Greek government and newspapers, to discourage emigration, published descriptions of the miseries of Greeks who had immigrated to the United States. The people of Greece, however, were not greatly dissuaded. Most of them began their great adventure knowing that they might fail but insisting on their right to try. They found passage money in any way they could: mortgaging their land, selling their livestock, using their savings, or borrowing from friends or relatives.

The great movement began in the region around Sparta in the early 1880s. From 1890 to 1910, an estimated three-fourths of the male population between the ages of 18 and 35 left Sparta; some went to the United States, others to Russia, Egypt, Turkey, or central Africa. After 1890, emigrants streamed out of nearly every part of Greece and the unredeemed lands. A drop in the price of currants, a major agricultural product of Greece, caused an exodus of farmers in the 1890s. Greeks who left Turkish-controlled areas usually did so for political reasons. When the new Turkish constitution of 1908 required military service of Greeks in Turkey, many left to avoid being drafted.

Although finding passage money may have been difficult in some cases, it was only the beginning of the troubles that many Greeks faced in their pursuit of a new life in America. Greeks were free to leave their own country without restriction, but many were turned back after they reached the United States because they could not pass the physical examination required for entry. The Greek government would not allow American health officials to operate in Greece, so prospective immigrants could not know whether they were healthy enough for entry until they had already crossed the ocean. The steamship companies lost money on the emigrants who were turned back, so these companies ultimately provided health inspections for those who purchased tickets. This made travel to America a bit more more secure for the Greeks.

Unlike many European immigrants who had been drawn to the New World by the promise of free land, very few Greek immigrants became farmers—despite their agricultural backgrounds. Since they usually planned a limited stay in America, not many were interested in the long-term investments of time and money required for farming. They went straight to the cities where they could find the help and companionship of other Greeks and the jobs and wages they sought.

Obstacles in America

The new arrival to the United States usually had the name of a city where he or she could find friends or relatives who were prepared to help. Although warmly welcomed as a newcomer from home, the new immigrant soon faced severe problems. Most acute was the matter of language. Very few Greek immigrants had any preparation in English at all. The vast differences between the two languages made it difficult for most Greek-speaking people to pick up English quickly. A typical new immigrant had to rely on other Greek immigrants who knew more, but often very little more, English than he or she did.

When it came to finding a job, the language barrier was a great handicap. In many cases it forced the immigrant to take the simplest kind of manual labor. But even if they had been more fluent in English, most immigrants would have had to take unskilled labor anyway. Coming as they did from rural backgrounds, they had no skills that could be applied to jobs in the cities. They began their hard climb to prosperity as railroad, construction, and maintenance workers, as day laborers, dishwashers, and bootblacks, or as street peddlers of fruits, vegetables, flowers, cigars, or candy. Some of these occupations provided a start for those who wanted to open their own businesses. Very little cash was needed to begin as a bootblack (someone who shines shoes) or peddler. By working harder than the competition and allowing themselves only the bare

Greek immigrants dressed up in national costume for International Night in Lowell, Massachusetts, in 1925.

The front page of the **Omaha Daily News** *tells of the 1909 anti-Greek riots in Omaha.*

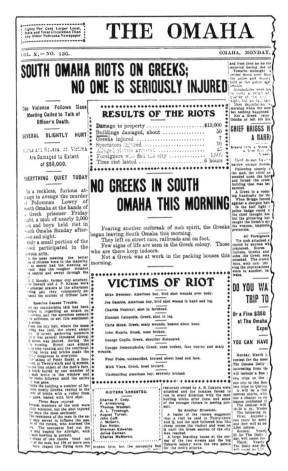

necessities of life, some successful Greeks were able to save enough to acquire shops of their own.

A large number of Greeks took up fishing in New England, Florida, and California. During the recession of 1893, many Greeks were forced out of peddling and into the textile mills of New England. A few professional people, especially doctors and lawyers, came to the United States, but they found the language barrier a fierce handicap.

Whatever the job, however, only the worst poverty could interrupt the flow of cash to those at home. The funds sent home were meant, first of all, to settle family debts, then perhaps to provide dowries or to pay passage for some other member of the family, and finally to be invested in the home neighborhood. A study of emigration made by the Greek government in 1906 showed that districts from which emigration was heaviest had become the most prosperous because of the money that the emigrants were sending home.

Greek immigrants soon found that they had to take a place at the bottom of the immigrant ladder. Other immigrant groups, though in the United States for only a slightly longer time, were still in a position to harass and

ridicule the Greeks. Because they knew so little English and so little about American law and customs, the Greeks were easy targets for anyone who wanted to trick them.

Whenever the economy slumped in America, people who could find no other reason for their financial troubles were happy to blame them on a group of strangers. If there was any shortage

33

With guitars and mandolins, young Greek men gathered for an afternoon of music in Lowell, Massachusetts, 1919. Groups such as this provided welcome diversion from the long work hours that were standard among Greek-Americans.

of jobs, the native labor force did not want to share the work with immigrant laborers. Being newcomers and having more than a little trouble with English, the Greeks usually knew nothing of the goals and methods of labor unions. The Greeks sometimes offended organized labor by working in factories after a strike had been called or by being willing to work for lower wages than other workers would accept.

Greeks faced all kinds of discrimination and opposition—from snubs and insults to violent anti-Greek riots. A severe disturbance took place in Omaha in 1909, when the Greek community of about 1,200 was driven from the city and its property was destroyed. Of course, every large group that entered the United States experienced much the same treatment, though that would have been no comfort to the Greeks

even if they had realized it. They were proud of their homeland and heritage and were anxious to correct the false opinions and unjust treatment that were so prevalent.

For most Greeks, the greatest problem of all was a feeling of loneliness and loss while working in a strange society. As hard as life had been in Greece, the consolations of an age-old order—of family, friends, church, coffeehouse, work, holidays—had softened the blow. The Greek immigrants to the United States, separated from the familiar routine of the village, longed for those simple comforts. Although they hoped for a place in American life, they wanted it as Greeks. Those with children wanted them to learn the Greek language and something about the homeland and cultural heritage of their parents.

The Padrones

Even harder to bear were the injustices that Greek immigrants suffered at the hands of other Greeks. As the number of Greeks in the United States grew, some of the more successful, following the example of American business, began to organize their enterprises into chains. Greeks had managed to succeed in the shoeshining business largely because they were willing to work harder and longer for smaller returns than their competitors. When a few began organizing chains of shoeshine parlors, their profits depended on a large supply of very cheap labor. Thus a padrone system, an exploitive labor-supply system already common within other immigrant groups, developed among the Greeks.

The laborers obtained by these padrones were really indentured servants similar to those in colonial America. The padrone or employer found his workers by contacting friends and relatives in Greece. Many families were eager to have their young sons, 14 to 18 years of age, go to the United States but were too poor to send them. The padrones offered to provide passage and transportation plus a small amount of cash in return for a boy's services for a specified time—anywhere from three months to one year. During this time the boy received board and room and was expected to work long, hard hours. The provisions were usually as meager as possible, and the work left the boys with no time or energy for recreation or school. The families of these boys had to give a guarantee equal to one year's wages to prevent them from breaking their contracts. Most families had to mortgage their property to provide such a guarantee.

After a year, the boys began to work at salaries of $10 to $20 a year. They might eventually average between $110 and $180 a year.

Neither the boys nor their families saw anything wrong with these arrangements. The families were happy to have the opportunity for their sons and considered the padrones their benefactors. Because the boys knew no English and depended upon the padrones for every kind of advice and information, they were unaware that they were being exploited. In addition, the pitiful salaries offered by the padrones seemed very desirable to impoverished people with no better prospects in Greece and no idea of normal American wages.

Gradually, American opinion rose against this system. Laws were passed to stop the practice and to punish the padrones, but the offenders had countless ways of escaping prosecution.

The padrone system finally died after enough boys realized they were being exploited and found better jobs on their own. Also, changing shoe styles and the increased use of automobiles brought a decline in the bootblack business. Aid societies were formed to help the bootblacks obtain better conditions, and eventually they even organized unions. Undoubtedly the increased understanding and independence of the immigrants themselves was the most important factor in putting the padrones out of business.

A Variety of Solutions

Greek-American Organizations

Like other immigrants, the Greeks gathered together in the cities where they could hope to find some security among other Greek immigrants. As one friend and relative followed another, these colonies of Greeks soon grew so large that some kind of organization seemed necessary to help the compatriots solve their problems. The first organizations formed by Greeks when they met far from home tended to be associations of those who came from the same town or village in Greece. These groups served as social clubs and as self-help societies. Each small association had a full set of officers, uniforms, and banners and took part in parades and civic functions. All this ceremony gave members a sense of importance they could not find elsewhere. These clubs raised funds for projects in their hometowns—schools, hospitals, bridges, relief after an earthquake, or assistance to widows and orphans. Often the priest or someone else from the home village in Greece would write to the members asking for help with a particular problem.

Rivalries among these associations wasted a great deal of energy and limited the amount of good they could do in their communities. To coordinate the activities of all Greek societies, the Panhellenic Union was formed in 1907. Soon, however, this society found conflict in its ranks. One side believed the union should help the Greek government reclaim the unredeemed lands. The other side wanted the society to help Greek immigrants help themselves in the United States, although they had no objection to helping Greeks at home on a personal basis.

Something new was added to the quarrel when a government official from Greece became the head of the Panhellenic Union. He had been sent to see that the group did what was of most use to the Greek government. When rumors began that the Greek government intended to tax the Greeks in America, the immigrants would not cooperate. Even after the union rid itself of foreign leadership, it often seemed more interested in the old country than in the new.

After the First World War, more and more immigrants realized that America would be their permanent home. More became naturalized, some as a result of having served in the U.S. armed forces during the war. Many immigrants who had returned to Greece to fight in the Balkan Wars came back to the United

States with their families and intended to stay. But their position was still uncomfortable in many ways. Americans became increasingly isolationist after the war, and aliens were still not welcome.

The American Hellenic Educational Progressive Association (AHEPA) was founded in 1922 to advance the Americanization of Greeks and to help combat unfavorable propaganda about them. The organization took the form of a fraternity. Its official language was English. No special attention was given to the Orthodox Church. In fact, many AHEPA members belonged to churches of other denominations.

For those who felt that AHEPA was too distracted by the anti-foreign feeling then prevalent in the United States, a new organization formed in 1923. The Greek American Progressive Association (GAPA) also assumed that the Greek immigrants were in America to stay. But GAPA's main concern was the Greek heritage, Greek language, and

The Hermes Social Club helped new Greek immigrants to prepare for American citizenship.

support for the Greek church. AHEPA, they thought, was abandoning these things. GAPA appealed to older and more conservative Greeks, but it was never able to match the membership of AHEPA.

Church

Of more immediate value to the Greek immigrant community was the organization of the *kinotitos*, or community council. This governing body promoted the establishment and financing of churches and schools and oversaw the election of officials and the hiring and firing of priests, teachers, and janitors. Once a Greek community reached a population of 500, it became eligible to have a kinotitos.

Because of the importance of the Orthodox Church as the center of community life in Greece, the establishment of a church was one of the first projects of interest to the Greek-American communities. People whose incomes were already stretched thin nonetheless found enough money to donate to church-establishment funds. Places of worship were either found or built in New York and Chicago in the early 1890s. Congregations in other cities were served by traveling priests. Between 1907 and 1909, however, churches were established in 10 more cities and, from 1914 to 1918, 61 more were organized. By the end of World War I, 130 Greek Orthodox

Athenagoras, the first Archbishop of North and South America

churches had been established in the United States.

Still, there was a shortage of trained clergy. Priests were brought from Greece, but many of them were simple clerics unequal to the complex duties of a city parish. Even many of those who were well educated were unable to adjust to American life or to give the kind of help the immigrant congregation needed.

The Eastern Orthodox Church is divided into several independent national churches, such as the Russian, Bulgarian, Cypriot, and Greek. Each has its own leader, known as its metropolitan or patriarch, but all are presided over by the supreme pontiff,

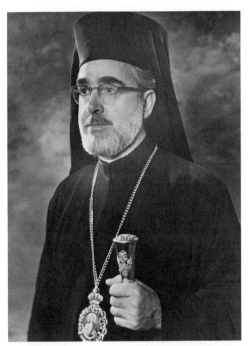

Iakavos, successor to Athenagoras as Archbishop of North and South America

the Ecumenical Patriarch of Constantinople. The Greeks in America wanted to be part of the Greek church, but the Greek hierarchy paid very little attention to the American church. Their representatives did not understand American problems or go to very great lengths to please Americans. Not until 1918 did the American church even have a bishop. The American church wanted and needed a workable administrative organization, authority over its own church, and facilities for educating its own clergy.

Finally, in 1930, the Ecumenical Patriarch of Constantinople took notice of the sad state of the American church. Passing over all the quarreling bishops and rival priests, he chose Athenagoras, the Metropolitan of Corfu (an island off the west coast of mainland Greece), to become the Archbishop of North and South America. Athenagoras began to reorganize administrative practices and to settle questions of authority that had been causing trouble for decades. He eliminated the other dioceses and made all the bishops directly responsible to him. He gave the clergy jurisdiction over all spiritual affairs and over such matters as the hiring of priests. To make Greek schools more successful, he tried to reorganize them with the church as the sponsoring organization.

Athenagoras also encouraged the churches to take drastic steps to deal with the financial difficulties caused by the Great Depression of the 1930s. He is responsible for lifting the Greek church in America from a mire of dissension and disorder and for giving it its identity as an American institution. The great importance attained by the American church was acknowledged when Athenagoras was elected Ecumenical Patriarch of Constantinople in 1948.

Greek Schools

The Greek schools were organized to provide the children of Greek immigrants with a knowledge of the language and culture their parents regarded so

39

Solon J. Vlasto, founder of **Atlantis***.
A strong voice for royalist politics,
the newspaper survived until 1972.*

Greek-Language Papers

The daily newspaper is a vital part of life in Greece, and it was inevitable that community life in the United States would give rise to Greek-language newspapers. The papers provided an opportunity to read Greek in a current and correct form. They formed a link, in the early days, between the Greek- and English-speaking communities. By subscribing to these newspapers, even those immigrants who spoke no English could keep informed of events in the cities that were their new homes. Greek-language papers also published much more news of Greece than was available elsewhere and provided American Greeks with material for their endless debates over Greek politics. These papers were an important link with home for the immigrant. They also helped in many cases to educate the immigrants in American customs.

Atlantis, founded in New York by Solon Vlasto in 1894, became a daily in 1904 and survived until 1972—longer than any other Greek-American newspaper. Supporting the views of the royalists, one of the two major political factions in Greece, *Atlantis* was somewhat ruthless in its treatment of papers that took the opposite stand. In 1915 the first successful liberal paper, the *National Herald (Ethnikos Kyrix)*, was founded in New York. Demetrios Callimachos, who served as its editor for 27 years, provided a voice for the liberal faction in Greece and was an

highly. The Greeks found, as did other immigrant groups with similar ambitions, that it was an uphill struggle. Qualified teachers were hard to find, as were funds with which to pay them. The children often resented attending Greek classes after their regular school day was over, and they resisted anything that seemed old-fashioned or strange or set them apart from their American friends. This was particularly true during periods of anti-Greek feeling. Gradually, in spite of anything their parents could do, the children born of immigrants in the United States became Americanized.

important force in shaping opinion in the Greek-American population. *Greek Star* (*Hellinikos Astir*), a Chicago-based paper, was founded in 1904. Almost all large Greek communities in America had a Greek-language paper for a time.

Coffeehouses

For the newly arrived immigrants, far from home and family, with very little money to spend on diversions, life could be very drab and lonely. Often, acquaintances would occupy a whole house together and take turns with housekeeping and cooking. Since most of the male workers planned to marry Greek women, they avoided the company of American women.

The coffeehouses in Greek neighborhoods were the logical solution to the problems of finding company and entertainment for these men. A familiar institution in Greece, a coffeehouse was inexpensive both to operate and to patronize. Here, for the price of a cup of thick Greek coffee, a man (and only men were allowed) could sit at a small table and smoke, read his paper, talk politics, and reminisce with friends for as long as he wished. Such a place filled a large gap in the lives of many lonely men.

Music, dancing, and cards were among the amusements available in the coffeehouses. Eventually, those in the larger cities could offer some other

*A Greek **taverna** on Rhodes. Tavernas and coffeehouses hold an important place in Greek village life and were replicated in the United States. Greek-American men could gather at such places for conversation and entertainment.*

modest entertainments. Traveling entertainers who could replicate the familiar Greek shadow plays performed in the coffeehouses. Sometimes, traveling strong men, musicians, or dancers were available. Usually the proprietor gave these performers board, room, and a small sum, and they were allowed to keep whatever the customers gave them after the performance.

But the coffeehouses drew criticism. They were a strange institution, and many non-Greeks misunderstood the violent political arguments they overheard there. Gambling became a problem in a few of the houses, and others suffered from the bad image this created. Eventually, as the family became the center of Greek-American social life, the coffeehouses began to disappear.

Repatriation

Of course, not all Greeks succeeded in the United States. Some continued to live in poverty. Some returned to Greece without either money or health. Before World War II, a fairly large proportion of Greek immigrants had gone back to Greece to live. Of those who came between 1908 and 1931, about 40 percent returned to Greece, mostly before 1925. They were repatriated for several different reasons and in several different ways. Some simply carried out their plan of improving their fortunes in order to return home. Many of these were able to make important contributions to Greek life. For instance, the first pasteurization plant in Athens was begun by a man who had learned the business and purchased his equipment in the United States. Others used know-how they had acquired in America to solve problems in their towns and villages. Some, even those who had quite a bit of money, found that they missed certain comforts and conveniences that they had grown used to in America.

Because of confusion in the laws regulating immigrants, some Greeks who planned to stay in America were drafted into the Greek army while they were visiting at home and never managed to get back again. Some who had gone back for a visit married women who did not want to leave Greece. Some of the repatriated Greeks remembered America fondly as a place where they would be if they could. Others remembered only that they had never worked so hard or been so miserable as they had been in America.

Turmoil in the Homeland

In the coffeehouses of Greek neighborhoods in the United States, customers heatedly debating political events in Greece had plenty to discuss.

During the Spanish-American War, 500 Cretans volunteered to fight against the Spanish in Cuba if the United States would provide passage for them. Their offer was refused even though it was meant as an expression of gratitude for the help Americans had given Greece during their War of Independence.

During the Balkan Wars (1912-1913), national feeling ran high among Greek-Americans and an amazing number volunteered to fight in Greece. Military units formed all over the United States and trained together. The Panhellenic Union acted as a recruiting agent and offended many people who thought it was improper for a foreign government to recruit in the United States. A total of 45,000 American volunteers served in the Balkan Wars.

The royalist-liberal debate in Greece divided the Greek-Americans into two political camps. The debate surfaced before the First World War, when the nations of the world were choosing sides in the growing conflict. King Constantine of Greece had been educated in Germany, had a German wife, and did not wish to offend Germany. He and his political supporters, the royalists, wanted Greece to stay out of the war and to remain completely neutral. The liberal party in Greece, led by Prime Minister Venizelos, wanted Greece to enter the war on the side of the Allies. (The United States supported the Allies even before it entered the war.)

From this time on, most Greek-Americans considered themselves either royalists or liberals (often called Venizelists) in political affairs both in Greece and in America. The royalists tended to take the Republican side in American politics. They preferred the aims of GAPA and were strong supporters of the Orthodox Church. The liberals usually supported the Democratic Party and the policies of AHEPA. They were less concerned with church affairs. With *Atlantis* and the *National Herald* leading the way, the Greeks in America argued each political problem from these two points of view.

The political problems in Greece and its late entry into World War I meant that Greeks in the United States who wanted to serve would have to join the American army. The Greek government tried to arrange to have Greek nationals serve as a unit under the Greek flag, but the United States would accept no such arrangement. A great many Greek-Americans did serve in the U.S. armed forces during World War I. A definite count is not available, but a good estimate based on the number of Greeks then living in the United States is about 60,000. One of them, George Dilboy, was awarded the Congressional Medal of Honor after his heroic death in the First World War. In addition, Greeks bought $30 million worth of liberty bonds.

Demetrios Callimachos, founder of the **National Herald**

43

In 1936 a military dictator, General Ioannis Metaxas (1871-1941), came to power in Greece. Most Greek-Americans were dismayed at this development in Greece especially at a time when Mussolini in Italy and Hitler in Germany were beginning to show their intentions. However, other Greek-Americans supported Metaxas because they felt that only such a strong government could deal with the problems of Greece. Both factions made serious efforts to win sympathy and support, but most Greek-Americans soon made it clear that they did not want Greece to support the Axis powers (Germany, Italy, and Japan).

When the Italians marched into Greece in 1940, everything changed. Metaxas and his successor led the Greeks in resisting the Italians. By using their old methods of mountain warfare, the Greeks were driving the Italians back when the great blow fell. In 1941, the Germans poured into Greece and quickly overcame the Greek forces and the 60,000 British troops who were assisting them. The Germans occupied both Greece and Crete as the king and his government fled into exile.

The occupation was a horror that can hardly be described. The country had already been weakened by the sacrifices it had made in resisting the Italians. When the German occupation authorities stopped vital imports of food and prohibited the export of food from one area of Greece to another, famine was the result. It was aggravated by the Nazi policies of commandeering anything they wanted and of taking reprisals against the Greeks for any acts of resistance. Once more, a Greek resistance movement organized in the mountains and continually harassed the Germans.

Ioannis Metaxas

44

Americans, along with much of the rest of the world, deeply admired the Greek resistance. Within two weeks of the invasion of Greece, the Greek War Relief Association (GWRA) had been formed in the United States with Spyros Skouras at its head. Working through local chapters of AHEPA, the GWRA sent requests for help to every segment of the Greek community. A few months later, President Roosevelt addressed these remarks to some members of AHEPA during their annual visit to the White House:

During the Hellenic war of independence more than a century ago, our young nation, prizing its own lately-won independence, expressed its ardent sympathy for the Greeks and hoped for Hellenic victory. The victory was achieved.

Today, at a far more perilous period in the history of Hellas, we intend to give full effect to our settled policy of extending all available material aid to a free people defending themselves against aggression. Such aid has been and will continue to be extended to Greece.

Whatever may be the temporary outcome of the present phase of the war . . . the people of Greece can count on the help and support of the government and people of the United States.

During its two and a half years of activity, the GWRA sent more than $100 million worth of food, clothing, medicine and other supplies to the citizens of Greece. Swedish vessels carried the goods, and a Red Cross commission saw that the goods were distributed only to Greeks. Many thousands of Greeks were saved by these supplies at the same time that thousands of others died of starvation and diseases related to malnutrition. Because the Nazis insisted that the source of the aid could not be revealed, the Greeks did not know until after the war that the supplies had come from the United States.

President Truman congratulates Christos Karaberis.

Greek prisoners of war interned by the Germans during World War II

When the United States entered the war, Greek-Americans turned their attention to the American war effort. In two great bond drives, the Greek-Americans contributed over $150 million. Many Americans of Greek descent served in the armed forces of the United States. One of them, Christos Karaberis, won the Congressional Medal of Honor for exceptional bravery in the Italian campaign.

In April of 1967, Greece faced its most serious political crisis since World War II. Led by Colonel George Papadopoulos, a group of military officers forcibly overthrew the constitutional government. Claiming that they were trying to prevent a Communist takeover of the government, Papadopoulos and his supporters quickly brought an end to democratic rule in Greece. Martial law was imposed, parliamentary rule was cancelled, all political activity was outlawed, and the Greek constitution of 1952 was suspended. Many basic civil rights and freedoms—including freedom of speech, the right of peaceful assembly, and freedom of the press—were taken away. Rigid limitations were placed on foreign travel. Other totalitarian restrictions were placed on the students and educators, the authors and journalists, the artists and actors of Greece. Several thousand political leaders and politically active citizens were arrested and imprisoned for speaking out against the military government, and thousands more were stripped of their Greek citizenship for leaving the country. At the same time, hundreds of private organizations were dissolved or put under tight government surveillance on the grounds that they were "subversive" or "suspect."

Among the prominent Greek citizens arrested for their political views and activities were former prime minister George Papandreou and his son, Andreas, a political leader as well as a university professor. The popular composer Mikis Theodorakis, who wrote the music for the film *Zorba the Greek*, was imprisoned, and his music was banned. In 1968, the world-famous actress Katina Paxinou, who won an Academy Award for her performance in the film *For Whom the Bell Tolls*, quit her position in the Greek National Theatre because of the strict limitations the government placed on the theatre. Melina Mercouri, a film star, was declared an enemy of the state and was denied her Greek citizenship after she spoke out against the military junta and left the country. Following in her footsteps, scores of other Greek artists who found it intolerable to live and work under government surveillance left the country to live in exile, becoming political refugees.

All of these developments and events were of special concern to the Greeks in America. Most Greek-Americans were vehemently opposed to the military government in Greece, and they hoped that it would be overthrown so that democracy could be reestablished. These sentiments were demonstrated by hundreds of Greek-Americans in 1968, during a Greek Liberation Parade held in New York City. The United States had to decide whether to treat the dictatorial junta as an outlaw government or to recognize the military regime and hope that it would

Melina Mercouri

hold free elections as it had promised. The United States government chose to recognize the new government early in 1968, after Papadopoulos had been in power for nine months.

In July of 1973, Papadopoulos was elected interim president of Greece—he was the only candidate—and voters approved a revised constitution that the dictator had proposed. Once elected to the presidency, Papadopoulos promised that a free and fair election would be held in 1974, and he removed a few high military officials from their governmental posts.

Fearing that its power would be further reduced, the Greek military overthrew Papadopoulos in November of 1973 and seized control of the government. The new military regime reintroduced some of the harshest repressive measures Greece had ever known, causing hundreds of persons to flee the country. The military government, however, found itself unable to run the country. So, in July of 1974, the military rulers resigned and turned the country back over to a civilian government, ending seven years of oppressive military rule in Greece.

Greeks in New York City protest the Papadopoulos dictatorship, 1968.

Andreas Papandreou, son of former Prime Minister George Papandreou, became prime minister of Greece in 1981.

The new civilian government moved swiftly to restore democratic rule to Greece, giving the people back their civil rights and individual liberties. Constantine Caramanlis, who had served as Greece's prime minister from 1955 to 1963, became head of the new government on July 24, 1974. Greece's first free elections in more than a decade were held in November 1974. Not surprisingly, Caramanlis and his New Democratic Party won. With the adoption of a new constitution in 1975, Greece officially became a republic. That same year, fallen dictator George Papadopoulos was convicted of treason and sentenced to death, but his sentence was later reduced to 25 years in prison.

In 1979, protests by Greek-Americans erupted in Astoria (New York), Washington, D.C., and other parts of the United States after President Jimmy Carter announced that the United States would resume supplying weapons to Turkey. Turkey had invaded the nation of Cyprus, a Mediterranean island with a Greek majority and a Turkish minority, in 1974. The Turks then created what is essentially a separate country, ruled by Turkish Cypriots, in the northern part of the island. This angered Greeks throughout the world and prompted the United

States to suspend military aid to Turkey for a few years, even though Turkey is a military ally of the United States. Even into the early 1990s, as Cyprus remained divided, Greek-American leaders continued to oppose U.S. military aid to Turkey and urged a full economic boycott.

Andreas Papandreou, a socialist, became prime minister of Greece in 1981. The son of George Papandreou, a former prime minister, he had been arrested along with his father during the Papadopoulos dictatorship.

Relations between the United States and Greece were strained, especially

49

A Greek immigrant displays some of the wares of the Corcoris sponge company in Tarpon Springs, Florida. Tarpon Springs, on the Gulf of Mexico just north of the mouth of Tampa Bay, has attracted numerous Greek immigrants.

in the early 1980s, as Papandreou's government threatened to withdraw from the North Atlantic Treaty Organization (NATO) and to close all U.S. military bases in Greece. The Greek government, fearful that Turkish forces might move against Greek territory, wanted the United States to reduce American military assistance to Turkey, which is also a member of NATO. The Papandreou government, however, never carried through on its threats. In 1989, Papandreou—whose personal life and financial dealings were clouded by numerous scandals—fell out of power and was replaced by an interim prime minister, Tzannis Tzannetakis.

Through all the political turmoil of the 1980s, however, and despite tensions between the governments of Greece and the United States, free contact between citizens of the two countries was never interrupted. Greek-Americans were free to visit Greece and Greeks were free to visit their relatives in the United States.

Survival of Hellenic Culture

Greek immigrants to the United States, like most other immigrants, felt a complex mixture of emotions toward their old homeland and toward their newly adopted country. After the First World War, many things worked to Americanize the Greek immigrant—the anti-foreign feeling after the war, the constant discussion in the Greek community about Americanization, and the work of such organizations as AHEPA. In addition, many Greek-American families had children who had been born in the United States and who did not want to be set apart in any way. A high point of naturalization was reached in the late 1920s.

The second generation, children of immigrants, did not want to be different from other Americans and tended to reject their parents' attempts to hellenize them. Even parents who only hoped that their children would keep their Greek names, follow their religion, and learn the Greek language were often disappointed. Many changed or Americanized their names. A large number left the Greek church for others, or for none at all. More and more Greek immigrants married Americans. Very few learned more than a little "household" Greek. A large number not only graduated from high school and college but obtained advanced degrees as well. Entering a variety of professions, most of them avoided the occupations of their parents.

The Second World War, however, marked another turning point. Partly because of widespread admiration for the Greek resistance to Hitler and Mussolini, a new attitude of pride developed among the younger Greek-Americans. They finally began to feel about their Greek heritage as their parents and grandparents hoped they might. They also began to recognize and take pride in the contributions made by other people of Greek descent to American life.

A Sunday picnic for Greek immigrants, Lowell, Massachusetts, 1920

4
CONTRIBUTIONS TO AMERICAN LIFE

Michael S. Dukakis

Greek immigrants and their descendants, by their personal industry and success as individuals, have made a generous contribution to American life. A number of them have won wide recognition for their outstanding achievements.

Government

In 1988, Michael S. Dukakis, a Democrat, became the first Greek-American to win a major party's endorsement for the presidency of the United States. Although he lost the election to George Bush, Dukakis carried 10 states (and the District of Columbia) and won more than 41 million votes. At the time he received his party's nomination for the presidency, Dukakis was serving his third term as governor of Massachusetts.

Numerous Americans of Greek descent have served in the U.S. Senate and the U.S. House of Representatives. Paul S. Sarbanes of Maryland (a Democrat) was first elected to the U.S. Senate in 1976 and was reelected in

1982 and 1988. He served on a select committee investigating secret military assistance to Iran and to the Nicaraguan Contras, and he was a member of the Senate Foreign Relations Committee and the Senate Housing and Urban Affairs Committee.

Olympia J. Snowe, a Republican from Maine, was first elected to the U.S. House of Representatives in 1978. She was the first Greek-American woman—and, at 31, the youngest Republican woman—ever elected to the U.S. House. Her father was born in Greece, as were her maternal grandparents. In 1990, she joined a majority of congresspersons in supporting a controversial bill requiring employers to grant time off without pay to workers who experience a family emergency.

Other members of the U.S. House of Representatives who are of Greek descent include Nicholas Mavroules of Massachusetts, George W. Gekas of Pennsylvania, and Michael Bilirakis of Florida—all of whom are Republicans.

Spiro Agnew, whose father was born in Greece, became the first person of Greek descent to serve as the governor of a U.S. state when he was elected governor of Maryland in 1966. Two years later he became the first Greek-American vice president of the United States. Agnew served for five years as vice president and was considered a leading presidential prospect until the U.S. Justice Department charged him with tax evasion. He pled no contest to the charges and resigned in 1973.

Olympia J. Snowe of Maine, the first Greek-American woman to serve in the U.S. Congress

Several persons of Greek descent have served as the mayors of large American cities. In 1987, Art Agnos was elected mayor of San Francisco, a city in which Greek-Americans have long played leadership roles. (George Christopher, a Greek immigrant, was San Francisco's mayor from 1955 to 1964.) The mayor of St. Paul, Minnesota, from 1960 to 1966 was George Vavoulis, and another Greek-American, Lee Alexander, was mayor of Syracuse, New York, in the 1970s.

BUSINESS

Even the earliest Greek immigrants were known for working long, hard days and for doing without many comforts while they struggled to establish themselves in business. As a result of their hard work, many Greek-Americans have become highly successful in commerce and industry.

Pindaros Roy Vagelos, whose parents were Greek immigrants, was born in New Jersey in 1929. Educated as a

Paul S. Sarbanes

54

biochemist and a medical doctor, he taught at Washington University in St. Louis for a few years before joining Merck & Company, one of the world's largest pharmaceutical firms, in 1975. By 1985 he had become chairperson, president, and chief executive officer of Merck. Besides his administrative achievements, the development of a technique to produce a cholesterol-inhibiting drug is credited to him.

The three Skouras brothers—Spyros, Charles, and George—came to America from the Peloponnesus. They worked at menial jobs until, in 1914, they had saved enough money to buy their first theater. In 1926, they owned 37 theaters in and around St. Louis. When the brothers sold their theaters to Warner Brothers, Spyros stayed on as an executive. In 1942 he left Warner Brothers to become the head of Twentieth Century Fox, where he remained until 1969. He also became chairman of the board of Prudential Lines, Inc., and, in 1966, president of Vessel Charters, Inc., of New York City. Spyros and his brothers did much to aid the relief efforts for Greece during and after World War II, and they contributed their time and money to a number of Greek-American organizations.

Thomas Pappas came to America as a child. Beginning with his father's grocery store, Pappas built up a chain of 35 stores and entered the importing and wholesaling businesses. After the Second World War, he sold these interests and invested in a great variety

Art Agnos, San Francisco's second Greek-American mayor

Thomas Pappas (right) started in business as a grocery-store owner. Maintaining strong ties to Greece, he served as U.S. ambassador to Athens and later helped establish a huge industrial complex in northern Greece.

Spyros Skouras (left), an executive in the film industry, also led numerous community-service campaigns. As head of the Greek War Relief Association, he helped ship food and medicine to Nazi-occupied Greece during World War II.

of enterprises. Active in Republican Party politics, Pappas was named U.S. ambassador to Greece during the Eisenhower administration. In the late 1960s, with the Standard Oil Company of New Jersey as a partner, Pappas oversaw the construction of a 200-million-dollar industrial complex in Thessaloniki, Greece. The eight companies in the complex produce steel, petroleum products, and numerous other important industrial materials. Pappas, who died in 1988, hoped to help make Greece self-sufficient in these products and to help revitalize the economy of northern Greece.

The Chicago-based Metron Steel Corporation is headed by Andrew Athens, a very active proponent of Greek-American political and social causes. Many Greeks, including New York shipowners George Livanos and Pericles Callimanopoulos, have been successful in the seafreight business. Entertainment entrepreneurs Sid and Marty Krofft, who created an indoor amusement park in Atlanta, Georgia, were the producers of a television variety show—*Donny and Marie*, starring Donny and Marie Osmond—that ran for several seasons in the 1970s.

Many Greeks in America have entered the restaurant business. Greek-American restaurateurs—many of whom are prominent businesspersons—have popularized such Greek specialties as *gyro* sandwiches, *souvlaki* (grilled pork kebabs), and the sweet dessert called *baklava*.

Pindaros Roy Vagelos

George Mylonas

Science and Education

While doing cancer research at the Cornell Medical Center in New York, Dr. George Papanicolaou (1883-1962) developed a smear test for detecting cervical cancer in women. The procedure, commonly known as the Pap smear, is simple and inexpensive and allows doctors to diagnose cervical cancer as much as 5 to 10 years before obvious symptoms would appear. This contribution by Dr. Papanicolau, who was born in Greece, has saved countless lives through early detection of cancer.

One of America's leading researchers in heart surgery is a Greek-American, Dr. John A. Elefteriades of the Yale University School of Medicine. A specialist in cardiothoracic surgery (surgery related to the heart and the entire chest cavity), Dr. Elefteriades is researching possible methods of using ordinary skeletal muscle to help weakened heart muscle continue to function.

Many of the leading scholars at United States universities were born in Greece. Moody Erasmus Prior, a professor of 17th- and 18th-century English literature at Northwestern University in Chicago, became a top Shakespeare scholar. In the late 1960s, he was appointed dean of graduate study at Northwestern University, where he later was honored as professor emeritus. Peter Charanis was a professor of Byzantine history at

Rutgers University and inspired greater interest in Byzantine studies in America. He died in 1985. Dimitri Tselos—a specialist in art of the Byzantine, early medieval, and modern periods—taught at New York University, Vassar, Bryn Mawr, and the University of Minnesota.

George Mylonas, a famous archaeologist, made major discoveries in 1952 about the Mycenaean civilization of Greece—the civilization that is famous for its war against Troy sometime before 1200 B.C. He published much material concerning the early burial shafts he discovered outside the citadel

Dr. George Papanicolaou of the Cornell Medical Center developed one of the most significant cancer-detection techniques in history. The Pap smear is a simple test that can reveal cervical cancer at a very early stage.

While in the U.S. Congress, John Brademas specialized in education legislation. He went on to head New York University.

at Mycenae, about other discoveries he made at Eleusis, and about archaeology in general. After his death in 1988, Mylonas was buried in Mycenae, on the Peloponnesus in Greece.

John Brademas, president of New York University, represented Indiana in the U.S. House of Representatives from 1959 to 1981. During his tenure in Congress, he concentrated on educational issues and was one of the cosponsors of the Elementary and Secondary Education Act of 1965. He was also one of the main forces in Congress urging a suspension of U.S. military aid to Turkey after Turkish forces invaded Cyprus in 1974.

Literature, Music, and Art

Nicholas Gage, a reporter and novelist, was born in Greece in 1939. (His family's original name is sometimes given as Gatzoyiannis, sometimes as Ngagoyeanes.) Gage was an investigative reporter for the *Washington Post* from 1967 to 1969 and for the *New York Times* from 1970 to 1980. While he was a reporter, he wrote a number of investigative books, including *The Mafia Is Not an Equal Opportunity Employer*. He then traveled to Greece to conduct a more personal investigation—into the circumstances surrounding the execution of his mother, Eleni Gatzoyiannis, by Greek Communists in 1948. In his

1983 book *Eleni*, Gage describes his search for the person who killed his mother and recreates the events in his home village of Lia that led up to her execution.

Eleni quickly became an influential book. In an address to the nation in December 1987, after having met with Mikhail Gorbachev, President Ronald Reagan quoted from *Eleni* and mentioned that Gage's story had made a

Nicholas Gage

Dr. John A. Elefteriades

deep impression on him. Reagan said that Eleni Gatzoyiannis's last words— "My children"—had inspired Reagan to seek peace for the sake of future generations. Gage published another book in 1989, *A Place for Us*, that follows up on some of the themes dealt with in *Eleni*. In 1990, Gage was presented with AHEPA's first-ever Herodotus Award to recognize his outstanding achievements.

Dimitri Mitropoulos

Another Greek-American writer is Harry Mark Petrakis, a novelist whose work focuses on the lives of Greeks in the United States. Two of his novels, *Lion at My Heart* (1959), and *A Dream of Kings* (1966), are set in the Greek community in Chicago, and his *Nick the Greek* (1979) is about Nicholas Dandolos, a famous gambler. Petrakis has also written two collections of short stories—*Pericles on 31st Street* (1965), and *The Waves of Night* (1969).

Maria Callas, one of the world's foremost coloratura sopranos (sopranos who specialize in highly embellished music), was born in New York City in 1923. Because her parents were Greek citizens, she was both a U.S. citizen and a citizen of Greece. Callas was trained in Italy and Greece and made her debut in Athens at the age of 14. She made her U.S. debut in 1954, winning critical acclaim for her brilliant singing and acting. The singer's

fiery temperament, her long association with the New York Metropolitan
Opera Company, and the virtuosity of
her performances in such technically
complex roles as that of Lucia in *Lucia
di Lammermoor* were legendary. Callas
gave up her U.S. citizenship in 1966,
but she returned to the United States
in 1974 for a highly successful concert
tour. She died in Paris in 1977.

One of the acknowledged masters
of classical music in the United States
was the Greek-born symphony conductor Dimitri Mitropoulos (1896-1960),
who came to the United States in 1936.
Mitropoulos conducted the Minneapolis Symphony from 1936 to 1949
and was principal conductor of the
New York Philharmonic Orchestra
until 1958. He also established a fund
to help aspiring young conductors.

Three Greek-American abstract
painters whose works are highly re-
spected in the contemporary art world
are Jean Xceron (1890-1968), William
Baziotes (1912-1963), and Theodoros
Stamos (born in 1922). During the
exciting days of the 1920s, Xceron
covered art news from Paris for American newspapers. He was born in
Greece, while Baziotes and Stamos
were both born in the United States.

John Vassos was an industrial de-
signer of Greek birth who came to the
United States in 1919. A talented artist
as well, he painted many murals. Vassos
designed the United States pavilion
for the Indian trade fair held in New
Delhi in 1955. He died in 1985.

Maria Callas

Olympia Dukakis, one of the leading actresses in the United States, founded the Whole Theatre Company–for stage productions–in New Jersey. She is best known, however, for her work in films. In 1988, she won an Academy Award as best supporting actress for the romantic comedy **Moonstruck***. She also starred in the 1989 film* **Steel Magnolias***.*

Entertainment and Sports

Elia Kazan, a leading director of plays and films, was born to Greek and Turkish parents in Istanbul, Turkey, in 1909. (His original family name was Kazanjoglous.) He and his family came to the United States in 1913 and settled in New York. His first major film, *A Tree Grows in Brooklyn* (1945), was a success, and many of his other films became American classics, including *A Streetcar Named Desire* (1951), *East of Eden* (1955), *Splendor in the Grass* (1961), and the two for which he won Academy Awards as best director—*Gentleman's Agreement* (1947) and *On the Waterfront* (1954). In 1987, Kazan won the D.W. Griffith Award from the Directors Guild of America. A gifted writer as well, Kazan has written such popular novels as *America, America* (1962), *The Arrangement* (1967), and *The Understudy* (1974), all three of which he has brought to the screen.

Melina Mercouri, a Greek film star, was introduced to America in the film *Never on Sunday*, for which she was named best actress at the Cannes Film Festival in 1960. She lived in the United States as a political refugee during the late 1960s, after she was stripped of her Greek citizenship for speaking out against the military junta that seized control of the Greek government in 1967. Mercouri returned to Greece in 1974, after the military government collapsed. She became a member of the Greek parliament in 1977 and served as the Greek government's Minister of Culture and Sciences.

Greek-American actor and director John Cassavetes (1929-1989) was a versatile and influential force in American cinema. He starred in such movies as *The Dirty Dozen* (1967), *Rosemary's Baby* (1968), and *Husbands* (1970, a film he also wrote and directed). His directing credits include such critically acclaimed films as *Faces* (1968), *A Woman Under the Influence* (1974), and *The Killing of a Chinese Bookie* (1976). Cassavetes was nominated for

Harry Mark Petrakis

65

Academy Awards three times—as best director for *A Woman Under the Influence*, as best writer for *Faces*, and as best supporting actor for *The Dirty Dozen*. He experimented with an innovative method of directing, by which the actors improvise the dialogue as they go along instead of memorizing a finished script.

Veteran Greek-American actor Telly Savalas won an Emmy Award in 1974 for his portrayal of a police inspector in the series *Kojak*. Although he is best-known as Kojak, Savalas also received an Academy Award nomination as best supporting actor in 1962 for his work in *The Birdman of Alcatraz*. Another Emmy winner of Greek descent is George Maharis, who received his award in 1962 for his performance in *Route 66*. Actor George Chakiris, another Greek-American, won an Academy Award as best supporting actor in 1961 for his performance in *West Side Story*. Chakiris also starred in *Squadron* (1964), *Is Paris Burning?* (1966), and many other films.

Two other television personalities of Greek ancestry are singer Tony Orlando and reporter Ike Pappas. In the 1970s, Orlando (whose full name is Michael Anthony Orlando Cassivitis) recorded such songs as "Knock Three Times" and "Tie a Yellow Ribbon 'Round the Old Oak Tree" and starred in the television variety show *Tony Orlando and Dawn*. Distinguished television reporter Ike Pappas, who worked for CBS from 1964 to 1988, often covered politics on the *CBS Evening News*.

Elia Kazan

Telly Savalas

Bill George (1930-1982), a linebacker, played professional football with the Chicago Bears and, for a year at the end of his career, with the Los Angeles Rams. He was voted All-Pro eight times and played on the Chicago team that won the world championship in 1963.

Alex Karras was a defensive tackle with the Detroit Lions who was born in 1939 to a Greek immigrant father and a Canadian mother. After a football career that included All-Pro distinction

Alex Karras

In professional baseball, Gus Triandos was a catcher for numerous teams—primarily the Baltimore Orioles and Philadelphia Phillies—from 1953 to 1965. He was known as a strong hitter and had three seasons of 20 or more home runs. Triandos was the catcher for Philadelphia during the perfect game that Jim Bunning pitched for the Phillies in 1964. Milt Pappas, another Greek-American, pitched for such teams as the Orioles, the Cincinnati Reds, and the Chicago Cubs in a career that spanned 17 seasons (1957-1973).

Two generations of leadership are represented by the late Mike N. Manatos (left) and his son Andrew. Mike Manatos, whose family is from Crete, became the first Greek-American to serve as a presidential assistant when President John F. Kennedy chose him to be liaison officer between the White House and the Senate. He later founded the lobbying firm of Manatos & Manatos, Inc., now headed by his son. Andrew E. Manatos continues his father's work in foreign policy issues—such as the division of Cyprus—that affect Greek-Americans. He has also served as an assistant secretary of commerce.

from 1960 through 1962, Karras went into broadcasting and acting. He worked for a while as a color commentator for ABC's *Monday Night Football* and eventually starred in a television sitcom called *Webster*. He also acted in several movies, including *Paper Lion*, based on the George Plimpton book about an amateur's attempts to play football with the Detroit Lions.

Greek-Americans are now firmly established in leadership positions throughout the United States. Having overcome poverty, prejudice, and numerous other hardships, they have succeeded through great tenacity and personal initiative. Greek-Americans have also demonstrated how valuable a close-knit community can be in solving the problems faced by new immigrants. They have succeeded as individuals, but many have also drawn strength from their identity as Greeks in America.

INDEX

AHEPA, 37-38, 43, 44, 51, 62
Agnew, Spiro, 53
Agnos, Art, 54, 55
Alexander, Lee, 54
Alexander the Great, 10, 11-12
Anagnos, Michael, 24, 25
archaeological findings about Greece, 21, 59-60
Athenagoras, Archbishop, 38, 39
Athens, 6, 10, 13, 42, 62
Athens, Andrew, 57

Balkan Wars, 7, 27, 42-43
Bilirakis, Michael, 53, 71
bootblacks, 32, 35-36
Brademas, John, 60
Byzantine Empire, 12, 13-14, 15, 28

Callas, Maria, 62-63
Cassavetes, John, 65-66
Chakiris, George, 66
Christopher, George, 54
classical period (Greek), 9-10, 23
coffeehouses, 41-42
Colvocoresses, George M., 23
Colvocoresses, George Partridge, 23
Cyprus, 4, 28, 49, 60

de Fuca, Juan, 17-19
Dukakis, Michael S., 52
Dukakis, Olympia, 64

Eastern Orthodox Church (*see also* Greek
    Orthodox Church), 14, 19
Elefteriades, John A., 58, 61
English language among Greeks, 32, 33, 35, 37, 40

farming: in America, 20, 31; in Greece, 9, 26, 29, 30

Gage, Nicholas, 60-62
GAPA, 37-38, 43
Gekas, George, 53
George, Bill, 67
George I, king of Greece, 26
Germany, 12, 43, 44, 45
Greece, geography of, 9, 27, 28
Greek language, 6, 8, 12, 37, 40, 51
Greek Orthodox Church, 21, 34, 38-39, 51
guerilla warfare in Greece, 20-21, 44-45

Howe, Dr. Samuel Gridley, 22, 24-25

Iakovos, Archbishop, 39
immigration: regulations, 7-8, 31; statistics for
    Greeks in U.S., 7, 8, 29, 30
independence, Greek, 20-22, 24, 25, 26-28

Juan de Fuca, Straits of, 17-19

Karras, Alex, 67-68
Kazan, Elia, 65, 66

Macedonia, 11, 12, 27, 28
Maharis, George, 66
Manatos, Andrew E., 68
Manatos, Mike N., 68
Mavroules, Nicholas, 2, 4, 53
Mercouri, Melina, 47, 65
Metaxas, Ioannis, 44
Miller, Col. Lucas Miltiades, 24, 25
Mitropoulos, Dimitri, 62, 63
Mylonas, George, 58, 59-60

Narváez, 16-17
newspapers (in Greek language), 40-41, 43
New Smyrna (Florida), 19-20, 21
Northwest Passage, 17, 18

Omaha (Nebraska), 33, 34
Orlando, Tony, 66
Otho, king of Greece, 26
Ottoman Empire, 14, 15

Panhellenic Union, 36
Papadopoulos, George, 46-49
Papandreou, Andreas, 47, 49-50
Papanicolaou, George, 58, 59
Pappas, Ike, 66
Pappas, Milt, 67
Pappas, Thomas, 57
Perkins Institute, 24, 25
Petrakis, Harry M., 62, 65
philhellenes, 6, 21, 22, 24-25
Philip II, king of Macedonia, 11
Plato, 6, 16
prejudice against Greeks, 8, 33-34, 37, 51

Roman Empire, 12-14
royalists, 40, 43
rural conditions in Greece, 26, 28, 29, 30, 31

Sarbanes, Paul S., 52-53, 54
Savalas, Telly, 66, 67
Skouras, Spyros, 45, 55, 56
Snowe, Olympia J., 53
Sophocles, Evangelinos Apostolides, 23-24
Sparta, 10, 29, 31

Triandos, Gus, 67
Turkey: Greek influence on, 11, 12; invasion of
    Cyprus by, 49, 60, 68; U.S. relations with, 22, 49,
    50, 68
Turnbull, Dr. Andrew, 18, 19-20

unredeemed lands, 28, 36

Vagelos, Pindaros R., 55, 57
Vassos, John, 63
Vavoulis, George, 54
Venizelists, 43

World War I, 36, 38, 43
World War II, 8, 42, 44-46, 51

Zachos, John, 24

ACKNOWLEDGMENTS The photographs in this book are reproduced through the courtesy of: p. 2, Nicholas Mavroules; p. 6, S.A. Johnson; p. 7, John DeMoss; pp. 9, 41, Greek National Tourist Office; p. 10, Louvre, Paris, Photo Alinari; p. 13, Steve Feinstein; pp. 14, 15, 72, Turkish Republic Ministry of Culture and Tourism; p. 16, Independent Picture Service; pp. 17, 19, 20, Dr. Carita Doggett Corse; p. 18, British Columbia Government; pp. 22, 24, Perkins School for the Blind; p. 23, Bureau of Naval Personnel, National Archives; p. 25, State Historical Society of Wisconsin; pp. 28, 29, *Greek Immigration to the United States,* Yale University Press; pp. 30, 32, 34, 37, 51, Theodore Koutras; p. 33, Nebraska State Historical Society; pp. 38, 39, Greek Orthodox Diocese of North and South America; p. 40, *Atlantis*; p. 43, Dr. Theodore Saloutas, *The Greeks in the United States*, Harvard University Press; p. 44, U.S. Information Agency, National Archives; p. 45, U.S. Army Photograph, Pentagon; p. 46, World War II Collection, National Archives; p. 47, United Artists Corporation; p. 48, New York *Tribune*; p. 49, Minneapolis *Star and Tribune*; p. 50, Library of Congress; p. 52, Michael S. Dukakis; p. 53, Olympia J. Snowe; p. 54, Paul Sarbanes; p. 55, Office of the Mayor of San Francisco; p. 56 (left) 20th Century-Fox Film Corporation; p. 56 (right) Standard Oil Company; p. 57, Merck & Company; p. 58, Herb Weitman, Washington University; p. 59, Barrett Gallagher for Cornell University Medical College; p. 60, New York University, Jill Krementz; p. 61 (left), Rey Alvarado; p. 61 (right), Nicholas Gage; p. 62, Minneapolis Symphony Orchestra; p. 63, Metropolitan Opera Archives; p. 64, 67 (left), Hollywood Book and Poster; p. 65, Herb Comess Photo; p. 66, Elia Kazan; p. 67 (right), Detroit Lions; p. 68 (left & right), Manatos & Manatos; p. 71, Mike Bilirakis.

Front cover photograph: Chris Kalogerson. Back cover photographs: Barrett Gallagher for Cornell University Medical College (left); Olympia J. Snowe (upper right); Nicholas Gage (lower right).

President George Bush signs a 1989 law co-sponsored by Rep. Michael Bilirakis (right), a Greek-American from Florida.

THE *IN AMERICA* SERIES

AMERICAN IMMIGRATION
THE **AMERICAN INDIAN,** VOL. I
THE **AMERICAN INDIAN,** VOL. II
THE **ARMENIANS**
THE **BLACKS**
THE **CHINESE**
THE **CZECHS & SLOVAKS**
THE **DANES**
THE **DUTCH**
THE **EAST INDIANS & PAKISTANIS**
THE **ENGLISH**
THE **FILIPINOS**
THE **FINNS**
THE **FRENCH**
THE **GERMANS**
THE **GREEKS**
THE **HUNGARIANS**

THE **IRISH**
THE **ITALIANS**
THE **JAPANESE**
THE **JEWS**
THE **KOREANS**
THE **LEBANESE**
THE **MEXICANS**
THE **NORWEGIANS**
THE **POLES**
THE **PUERTO RICANS**
THE **RUSSIANS**
THE **SCOTS & SCOTCH-IRISH**
THE **SWEDES**
THE **UKRAINIANS**
THE **VIETNAMESE**
THE **YUGOSLAVS**

Lerner Publications Company
241 First Avenue North · Minneapolis, Minnesota 55401